Wellington and The Wrekin
in old picture postcards

Wellington and The Wrekin
in old picture postcards

by George Evans

European Library ZALTBOMMEL/THE NETHERLANDS

Acknowledgements
I am most grateful to Councillor Philip Morris-Jones, Mrs. Audrey Smith, Mr. Bill Bayley and Mr. Frank Edwards for the loan of postcards and other photographs; to Reverend Dr. Harry Foreman, the Victoria County History, the Local Studies library, the writers of various guidebooks and many friends for information and help. In particular I must thank my wife for her advice, encouragement, typing and patience.

Sources, where known:
R.M. & S., Shrewsbury, Princess Series; Caption, 81.
R.M. & S., Shrewsbury, Cleveland Series; 14.
Valentine; 3, 4, 21, 30, 40, 78, 82, 84.
The Wrench Series; 5.
W. Frith & Co., Reigate; 6, 16, 18, 19, 48, 51.
Milton 'Elite-Glazette'; 7, 33, 52.
K. Ltd.; 53
Scottish Photographic Touring and Picture Post Card Co., Glasgow; 54, 56.
Tom Austin, Wellington; 67.
Hobson & Co., Wellington; 83.

GB ISBN 90 288 4564 x

Second edition, 1999: reprint of the original edition of 1987.

INTRODUCTION

The purpose of this book is to show, using old picture postcards produced at the time, an important part of the history of Wellington. The period we are looking at is from 1880 to 1930. These fifty years, mostly within the memory of many people still living in the town, were an interesting period of British history, comprising the later years of Queen Victoria and the reigns of Edward VII and George V. They were certainly exciting enough for the people of Wellington.

During the time we are concerned with Wellington was a thriving market town, second only within Shropshire to its younger rival, Shrewsbury. It lay at the foot of The Wrekin and on the edge of the industrial area of the East Shropshire coalfield where the Industrial Revolution had been born over a century earlier. It was the major communications centre for East Shropshire and bustled with industry and commerce.

Wellington is older than Shropshire. Its name implies a heathen temple in a grove, from which we can suppose that it was founded before the days of Offa, King of Mercia, who was a Christian. It has been suggested that Wellington was founded by Saxons whose ancestors had been mercenaries employed by the Romans and Romanised Britons of Viroconium, the city near Wroxeter. The city had been abandoned following a great plague over 1,440 years ago. The heathen temple would have been replaced by a cross and eventually by All Saints' Church. By Domesday there was a resident priest.

Markets were held at first on the Green to the north of the churchyard and moved to a larger site south of the church when a Charter was granted by Edward I to the Lord of the Manor, Giles de Erdington. This new site included Crown Street, Bell Street, Duke Street and the present Market Square. New Street was built around this time and laid out with burgage plots on each side. Medieval crafts included cloth processing and leather manufacture. There were many Lords of the Manor but most of them lived out of the town.

Until the 18th century all the buildings were of timber; they were afterwards bricked over or replaced. There was a wooden Market Hall in the Square with a court room upstairs for the South Bradford Magistrates. The cloth trade was once important; evidence still exists in place names: Walker Street (fulling) and Ten Tree Croft – Tenter Croft – where the dyed cloth was hung to dry on tenterhooks. The invention of a water powered fulling mill must have caused a decline in trade as there was no river to provide the power.

During the Civil War King Charles I mustered his army in Orleton Park but later Cromwell's men captured Apley Castle and All Saints' Church causing much damage. They were driven out by local Royalists.

As the coalfields in the parish – at Ketley and Hadley and neighbouring Dawley, Madeley and Coalbrookdale – grew, Wellington expanded. Houses in town were replaced by shops and wealthier traders moved to the outskirts. At one time there were serious market riots for which some men were executed. Trades included nail and bell making and especially wooden furniture. Some workers were very poor; many tiny cottages were built and a Union Workhouse in Walker Street. The railway arrived in 1849 and Wellington became an important junction, bringing an expansion of trade in coal, timber, livestock, brewing and malting and an important carriage works.

There were two railway stations; a passenger station in Station Road and a goods depot in Bridge Road with sidings, cattle pens, coal wharf and other facilities. Both stations were joint G.W.R./L.M.S. operated. The passenger station had coaling and water facilities, turntable and a repair shed with three main platforms and a bay containing two more platforms for local services. Originally refreshments were provided outside the station at what is now the Station Hotel but later there were two refreshment rooms on the station itself.

Local banks and a newspaper – the Wellington Journal – sprang up. More churches, for Baptists, Congregationalists, Methodists and Roman Catholics together with an additional Anglican church – Christ Church – were built. Most of the old Market Place had filled with shops and inns and the newly formed Markets Company bought the Charter rights from the Lord of the Manor, Lord Forester, and built a new Market Hall, Potato Market and Corn Exchange. The Monday livestock market, held at the Smithfield, became a thriving business.

There was a great number of public houses and a good deal of drunkenness. A gas works began in Tan Bank followed by electricity supply. Toys and dolls were made at three factories and bread ovens at another.

Dr. William Withering, a local physician, discovered a medicine, the principal constitutant of which was foxgloves on sale in the market. He popularised its use as digitalis for the treatment of heart complaints. He also campaigned for the abolition of slavery.

Sarah Smith, who under her pen name Hesba Stretton was an early best selling authoress, wrote 'Jessica's First Prayer' and other 'improving' Victorian romances.

John Crump Bowring of Bradley Moor made a small fortune as a fish dealer and became a local benefactor, giving the Bowring Recreation Ground and the church gates to the town. His widow was the principal patron of the Cottage Hospital. O.D. Murphy founded the Wrekin Brewery and the Mineral Water Works and his widow gave a playing field in Oreleton Lane to the people of Wellington. The Corbett family were ironfounders and left an interesting iron tomb near All Saints'. Sir John Bayley founded Wellington College which became Wrekin College. Dr. Cranage founded the Old Hall School and was active very early in the ecumenical movement.

Wellington Urban District Council was faced with a great slum clearance problem at the turn of the century. A great many small houses had been built hastily in Nailors Row, Chapel Street, Parton Square and High Street which were now fit only for demolition. The Council began building in 1902 and eventually completed over 2,000 dwellings. Their plans for developing the town, however, were frustrated by local government reorganisation in 1974 and the coming of Telford.

The Wrekin has always been of great importance to the people of Wellington – first as a refuge, then as a forest, now for recreation. It is regarded as 'our hill' and the local toast is to All Friends Round The Wrekin. It is no wonder that many local postcards featured The Wrekin as a reminder to friends and family of the local landmark. The two main refreshment places, the Forest Glen Pavilion of the Pointon family and Wrekin Cottage, were much loved for family outings.

Modern Wellington remains a friendly market town of around 18,000 people, well served by shops, schools and most services – and especially by its market.

1. Many picture postcards of Wellington depict the Market Square or Market Place as it is sometimes called. This one looks from Church Street; the photographer is on the railway bridge with his back to the church. Although superficially similar to today's view from the same point, on careful consideration many differences can be detected in the uses of buildings as well as the clothing of the people. This postcard was also produced in a coloured form. The shop advertising J.W. Owen, clothier, was a gentlemen's outfitter though in later pictures it will be seen as Walter Davies with a similar business. The Market Hall which used to stand in the Square in 1680 had been dismantled and sold about 1800.

2. Looking in the opposite direction at about the same time – is it the same boy on the left? Behind the ornamental gas lamp is the Wrekin Hotel, the ground floor of which is replaced by shops in later views. Over the shop on the right of this hotel, on the other side of the narrow entrance to Market Street, lived Dr. Pooler who, in his autobiography, described many events he had witnessed from his bedroom window as a boy. These included a military band playing in the Square while the officers were at dinner in the hotel and bear-baiting when dogs were set to attack a bear. He also describes the celebrations to welcome Captain Matthew Webb after his successful attempt to be first to swim the English Channel.

3. A similar view by Valentines looks up Church Street with many buildings which are now demolished on the left hand side of the street. These include Lloyds Bank, an imposing stone faced building in this picture. Facing us in the distance is the old Post Office. The shops on the right include a ladies' fashion shop called Capsey's where dresses were made in a workroom above. A young apprentice in 1903, Mabel Fail, was given five shillings in appreciation for her first year's work. The shop on the extreme right was Baxters. Mr. Baxter used to stand facing the entrance and when a customer entered he would order 'forward' and an assistant would come immediately ready to serve.

4. In the centre of this picture is the old post office which had superseded an earlier timber framed building in New Street and was later to be replaced by a further building in Walker Street. The large tubular posting box outside is the only remaining clue that this was once the post office. The remainder of the building was the printing and publishing premises of The Wellington Journal and Shrewsbury News founded by Thomas Leake in 1854. The trees are in the churchyard on the site occupied in 1918 and since by the lychgate built as a memorial to the local men who gave their lives in the Great War.

5. Bandsmen of the King's Shropshire Light Infantry are here seen with their instruments coming from Station Road. The K.S.L.I. and the Shropshire Yeomanry, a cavalry regiment, played an important part in the life of the town. A battery of the 1st Shropshire and Staffordshire Artillery Volunteers used the Drill Hall in King Street as their headquarters. The North and South Wales Bank is now the Midland Bank. Boots, advertising themselves here as the largest chemists in the world, had their shop behind J.W. Owen, facing Crown Street on one side and Duke Street on the other. They have since moved to New Street. The window of J.W. Owen's shop facing New Street was often broken by the post coach rounding the sharp corner in a hurry, heading for the post office shown in picture 4. Bollards were placed to protect the window though they have since been removed.

6. By the time this photograph was taken J.W. Owen had sold No. 1. The Square to Walter Davies who carried on a similar business, presumably after retiling the roof. It will be noticed that the gable over the middle window of this building does not fit the window. The Duke Street front of Boots the Chemist can be clearly seen although the large sign above has disappeared. The bow fronted building on the right was always known as Slaney's Vaults. A shoe shop has taken over the market street side of the Wrekin Hotel which became a Temperance Hotel. Mr. Cooke of Cooke's Provisions, on the left of Walter Davies' and at the bottom of New Street sold groceries of all kinds and was a prominent member of the Rechabite movement, a temperance society.

7. Woolstone Bros. of London produced this 'framed' picture of the Market Square for the Milton 'Elite Glazette' series. It is quite elaborate; the frame is embossed and relatively large. Like many cards of its day this one was used, in 1912, to announce a safe arrival. Until the Great War the Square was the scene of an annual Gauby Market, held on the first Thursday after Christmas. Young lads came to be hired for the year by farmers. Any lad who wanted to be hired would keep a straw in his mouth which was removed by the farmer as a signal that he was hired. The largest shop to be seen is Capsey's where many local ladies went to have dresses made to order. The workshops in which the dressmakers worked were behind the shop.

8. The interior of a ladies' dress shop is shown here at the turn of the century in an unusual photograph. Customers are being solicitously attended by shop assistants; there is plenty of competition next door. All the customers can be seen to be wearing hats. The walls are lined with boxes and cardboard drawers of goods for sale. Chairs are provided for customers though an assistant would not like to be caught sitting. It is clearly a busy day. Any garment could be altered in size or style or made to measure very quickly by seamstresses working upstairs. The latest styles in patterns were always available and these could be readily modified to suit the figure or whims of the customer, who was, it should never be forgotten, 'always right'.

9. Further back in the shop customers are invited to examine lengths of cloth of various materials and patterns. Many of the customers made their own clothes and would come to the shop to purchase materials and patterns. The patterns would be of paper and would help to ensure that the dress was fashionable and stylish. All this took a great deal of time. Clothing for all the family was often made at home by busy mothers working in the evening. In the shop is provided a great variety of cloths which would be ordered by the yard – dresslengths of various sizes. The cloth was measured either with a yardstick or against a brass ruler set in the counter. It was cut off with a large pair of scissors. Needles and thread were bought at the same shop, also ribbons, lace, buttons and other sewing necessities.

10. Here we see the inside of the sewing room above the back of the shop. Girls would begin work here as apprentices as soon as they had left school at the age of fourteen. They would start at eight in the morning and work until six o'clock in the evening. It was a long day but unlike their contemporaries who 'went into service' they would be lucky enough to get every Sunday off. It was hard work and they were closely supervised but in this workshop the atmosphere was friendly and the training was very valuable even if they left to get married, which most of them did. Some of the girls set up in business on their own after 'serving their time' in this sort of shop and became dressmakers on their own account.

11. The Square is seen from Church Street in Edwardian times. Brittain's two shops on the right were on each side of Slaney's Vaults, a public house. The nearest one in the picture sold cakes and had a tea room and restaurant at the back of the shop and on the first floor. It had a very appetising smell. The upstairs restaurant had, as can be seen in the picture, a large window overlooking the street. There were waitresses in uniform to serve customers. The further shop was a grocers and had sides of bacon hanging up ready to be cut to whatever thickness was required. Customers would sit on high chairs at the counter while assistants would scurry round the shop with customer's lists of items. Facing us are Crown Street and Duke Street, part of the 13th century Market Place but built up by the 18th century leaving only the small part now called The Square open except for the Market House.

12. The shop on the left is Hobson's, selling stationery and also taking orders for printing. Hobson's did a great deal of the printing for the town and district. Robert Hobson started the town's first newspaper in 1849. Hobson's also sold books and artists' materials such as watercolours and oil paints. The printing works was detached from the shop, next to the market hall. Adjoining Hobson's was the Wrekin Hotel which by this time was a temperance hotel. The window above the entrance was used at various times for the declaration of poll. Election results were announced to crowds waiting in The Square. The outer casing of this window has now been removed to make way for the sign of Stead and Simpson's shop.

13. On the right of this picture it is clear that another side of the Wrekin Hotel has been taken over by a jeweller's shop – Scotts, leaving only the entrance on the ground floor facing The Square. The old timber framed building facing us, Walter Davies Complete Gentleman's Outfitter, sold all the clothing needed for men and boys. Most of the men's suits were tailor made though shirts may well have been made and socks knitted by their wives. A suit could be bought for around £2.10s. and would last for many years. The shop is probably the oldest in the town and the remains of a market stall which grew into a shop. There are many postcards of the Market Square in Wellington because it is the commercial heart of the town. The 17th century Market House stood in the centre of the Square until 1804 when it was dismantled and sold. It was constructed of timber, having a court room upstairs supported on pillars, leaving the ground floor open and measured 18 feet by 36 feet. General markets were held in the street until 1866.

29432 THE SQUARE WELLINGTON.

14. Here we see almost exactly the same scene in the late 1920's on a postcard of the 'Cleveland' series by R.M. & S. Ltd. The Square, about ten years later was the scene of a 'riot' when Sir Oswald Mosely and his blackshirts came to seek support. Eggs and tomatoes were thrown at them from the windows above Lloyds the grocers on the left. Sir Oswald's car was overturned in front of Walter Davies' shop. The Square was thronged with angry Wellingtonians. The meeting broke up in considerable disorder. In the 1920's Perks' Stores – a grocers – used to have a Trojan van with solid tyres which would deliver groceries for customers. Perks and Hepworth's in this picture have taken over Capsey's shop. Both have now gone but the building remains.

15. This old photograph shows the three shops next to the railway bridge. All three buildings have now gone and are replaced by John Menzies. Mr. Bert Richards, who had previously had a shop on the Green, used to sell tobacco from jars and would blend different types to suit his customers, wrapping up an ounce in a conical white paper bag. He sold many kinds of cigarettes including Balkan and Turkish; De Reszke cigarettes had coupons which could be collected to exchange for wireless sets and gramophones. Like other tobacconists he also sold walking sticks and umbrellas. The ladies' and gentlemen's hairdressing salons were entirely separate from each other. Nobletts was a most delightful sweet shop, very popular with children; liquorice, sherbert and toffee were sold for a halfpenny or a farthing.

16. This Frith's postcard says Market Square but in fact is a picture of Church Street. The photographer has his back to the Market Square and the churchyard can be seen on the right. Straight ahead is the post office which was here until it was moved to a new site in Walker Street in 1927. Since then, for many years the premises was Agnews, a ladies' and gentleman's clothing shop. The imposing front of Lloyd's Bank has now been replaced by a much simpler modern building. The bank started as the Shropshire Banking Company and was taken over by Lloyd's Banking Co. Ltd. in 1874. On the left is Smith's Vaults, now The Bacchus. Just before the bank is a narrow alleyway now called Ten Tree Croft, derived from the field name Tenter Croft, where dyers hung out their cloth on tenterhooks to dry. Between the bank and the post office was the ironmongery business of S. Corbett & Son, later W. Corbett & Co., who by 1909 were making galvanised iron tanks in Alexandra Road and Mr. Arnold was selling suitcases, satchels and other leather goods at this shop .

17. Here is Church Street again, rather further up the street. To the right of the post office is John Jones and the rest of the building and round into Queen Street was taken up by the Wellington Journal. In 1854 Thomas Leake founded the Wellington Journal and Shrewsbury News. Its circulation grew from 4,550 in 1864 to 40,000 by 1900 and 48,000 in 1965 when it lost its independence and was moved to Ketley. In its heyday the Wellington Journal was highly respected throughout Shropshire and bordering counties. The Leake family continued all this time to own the Journal which tended towards conservatism and absorbed its liberal rival The Wellington Standard. In addition to local and national news The Journal published fat stock prices at several auctions and so was essential reading for local farmers.

18. Barclay's Bank, a fine ornamental building, has now been replaced by a very plain edifice of little character. It was discovered to be on quicksand and pile driving went on day and night for its replacement. The inscription of the original bankers, Birmingham, District and Counties Bank can be seen above the first floor. On the right is The Green, or what remains of it, the site of the market place before Giles de Erdington moved it in 1244 to the present Square. Here it was on the north side of the churchyard. It is now used only as a car park. In the distance is the Charlton Arms Hotel – now much enlarged. Beyond that can be seen the gable end of the police station which incorporated the Magistrates' Courts, the Police Inspector's house and the lock-up. It was built in 1897 to replace former premises seen here near The Green with arched entrances.

19. Looking across The Green as it used to be we see the Church of All Saints built in 1790 to replace a much earlier church. This site was probably the original focus of Wellington in Anglo-Saxon times, first as the temple within the grove which gave the settlement its name and later, in Christian times, the churchyard. Early highways into the town terminated at The Green, the original market place where visitors to the church naturally congregated. Before the Great War there was a maypole here, with dancing on Lady Day. The photograph shows the iron gates given by John Crump Bowring, a local merchant, who also gave the Bowring Recreation Ground opposite his house, Bradley Moor, in Haygate Road. His widow was the principal donor of the Cottage Hospital. Just to the right of the gates is the site of the former lock-up of 1779. The building on the left has been demolished to make way for the National Provincial Bank – now the National Westminster.

20. 'The Priory' was built originally as a vicarage for All Saints' Church. One of the vicars who lived there, Reverend A.Z. Grace, is reputed to have 'lost five children from diphtheria, became ill and took to drink'. Another vicar, Reverend H.M. Marsh-Edwards, resigned in 1901 before his liaison with a servant-girl became public knowledge. He gave notice to quit to a tenant in one of the lodges attached to the vicarage because the tenant was a Methodist and did not attend church. When a new vicarage was built in Haygate Road, this house was sold and was the home of the Chubb family and called The Priory. Later it was bought by a builder, used as a Services Club and eventually demolished to make room for Priory Close.

21. Wellington Church – All Saints – from a postcard of 1906; this is a Valentines card showing the church designed in 1790 by George Steuart who later built Attingham and St. Chad's Church, Shrewsbury. It is built of stone in the classical style, consisting of an aisled nave of five bays with eastern apse. The west front, seen here with its three bays and Tuscan pilasters, is surmounted by a square tower with a domed roof. There are five bells from the old church, three later bells; one dated 1798 and two dated 1890. The galleries are supported by iron columns, sometimes supposed to be the earliest made. These were originally exposed but are now plastered and 'marbled'. Nikolaus Pevsner in 'The Buildings of England', having complained that Wellington is 'depressingly poor in works of architectural value' describes the church as 'a fine dignified stone building – presented far too self-consciously'.

22. Seen over the wall of the churchyard is the railway passenger station in its deep cutting. The line was opened to Shrewsbury in 1849 jointly by the Shrewsbury and Birmingham Railway Co. (later G.W.R.) and the Shropshire Union Railways and Canal Co. (later L.N.W.R. and still later L.M.S.). The same year lines were opened to Wolverhampton and to Stafford. By 1867 branch lines to the coalfield townships gave direct services to Coalbrookdale, Much Wenlock and Craven Arms. In the same year the Wellington-Market Drayton line was opened. All this made Wellington a most important railway junction and contributed to the town's prosperity. Until British Rail was formed there was considerable rivalry between G.W.R. and L.M.S. staff.

23. Station Road was built to connect the passenger station (there was a goods station in Bridge Road) with the centre of the town when the line was opened in 1849. The building on the right is the Station Hotel which was originally built as a station buffet. It is a very narrow building indeed and nothing like as large as its imposing façade suggests. Until the 1930's there were 'drays' each pulled by two huge shire horses bringing goods to and from the parcel office to the right of the station entrance. The station is on the site of a previous vicarage. Surmounting the main building can be seen a cross and other crosses were built into the ironwork, roof supports, gates and water pipes. It is sometimes supposed that this is because part of the burial ground was used for the station and bodies were removed when the cutting was dug.

24. In its heyday Wellington was a very busy junction indeed. It was jointly owned and run by the Great Western and London Midland and Scottish Railways. The picture shows a Great Western train on the 'up' line (to London). Above the engine is a large water tank. Behind the carriages were engine and coal sheds and a hand operated turntable. Through trains (mainly goods) used the two centre lines. Behind the camera were two 'bays' which were used for local lines with small stopping trains such as the 'Ketley Dodger'. A slip coach was employed at one time. A water trough between the rails enabled engines to pick up water at speed through a syphon. Some trains had names such as the Zulu, so called because it had brought news of the end of the Zulu war.

25. This photograph shows the dovecote at Dothill. There are very few available pictures of the house at Dothill which is now long gone. Dothill was one of Wellington's berewicks in 1086. By the later middle ages it belonged to the Steventon family and was a large house enclosed within a moat. The Forester family owned it for some time until by 1922 the chief landowner was Ernest Groom, a timber merchant. Groom's Yard, next to the goods station, was at one time the country's largest timber business. It is now a car park and a motor repair business. Almost all of Dothill is now covered over in houses since the Urban Council acquired the land from Mr. H.F. Hodgson in 1956. Early drawings show the house as a five bayed north-south range entered from the east, incorporating a three bayed hall. Dovecotes like this one were common to manor houses and provided fresh meat from the 'squabs' or young doves in winter when other fresh meat was unobtainable.

26. Apley Castle, shown here, is the house designed by Joseph Bromfield and built 1792-1794. It was subsequently greatly enlarged in 1856 but the side we see in the photograph is the older north-west front. The whole house was demolished in 1955 and the portico seen in the picture is now near Hodnet Hall. After 1856 St. John Chiverton Charlton had many trees planted in the gardens which are now a public arboretum. An earlier castle built in 1327 and enlarged in the early 17th century still stands having been used since 1794 as a stable block but is now derelict. The old castle suffered damage after capture by royalist forces in 1644. The Charlton family, who had lived at Apley since the 14th century are commemorated by the Charlton Arms Hotel. Charlton Street and Charlton school. The lake shown was used for skating in the winter.

27. All Saints' Church is seen here on a large glass plate photograph. The plate was discovered recently among the goods left by Mr. 'Rocker' Shaw the jeweller of New Street. He may well have taken the photograph. All the tombstones shown here have been removed to make the parish church garden by the Urban Council in the late 1950's. Most of the stones were placed around the boundary of the new garden which was grassed over. The large tomb in the left foreground, however, belongs to the Corbett family who by the 1870's had a flourishing agricultural machinery business. It is a cast iron tomb and now is on the south side of the church. The Corbetts were agricultural implement makers of Park Street and in the 1890's among the country's best known manufacturers of agricultural machinery competing locally with Haynes & Bromley, later John Bromley & Co.

28. The old church shown here in a drawing was demolished in 1787. At least one window dated from the 12th century. This view is from the east. The north and south aisles were probably added in the 15th century; the east chancel window was 14th century. This church was damaged during the civil war action when it was captured with Apley Castle by parliamentarians and subsequently retaken by Royalists. The new church was built on the east side of the old church so the tombstones shown in the last picture are in the place where the church stands here. The building on the right may be the grammar school.

29. The photograph here shows the Square after the great parade which celebrated the coronation of King Edward VII in 1902. The litter, some of it due to horses, shows that the parade is over. The saluting dais can be seen in front of the Wrekin Hotel. Some of the shopkeepers have boarded up their windows to protect them from the crush. For this celebration a resident of Victoria Avenue, manager of the Castle Works at Hadley, erected a display of electric lights with portraits of the King and Queen Alexandra. The library in Walker Street was opened to celebrate the coronation.

30. This Valentines postcard shows the bottom end of New Street. The street was new in 1244 with the first market charter. Bell Street, on the right, was formerly Swinemarket and was part of the original market square. Espley's, the pork butchers, had a slaughter house in Bell Street to supply their shop in New Street. Most of the shops had living accommodation above them and long gardens at the back, having been laid out as burgess plots in the 13th century. The street is still as narrow as it is shown in the photograph but many of the quite substantial buildings are now gone, replaced by modern shops on the same site. Many of the shops in the photograph, however, have replaced older, wooden framed buildings or are brick façades.

31. Mr. Tom Shaw, nicknamed 'Rocker' Shaw is seen here proudly standing in front of his shop in New Street. The photograph was taken on a glass plate by Mr. Cooper-Edmonds who had a photographic business in town. It will be noted that the trade of optician went together with the jewellery and watch trade. Mr. Shaw was a well-known and rather dashing figure in the town and had one of the first cars. Looking at the shop it can be seen that it was not thought necessary to take any elaborate precautions to protect its valuable contents.

32. This plate photograph was probably by Mr. Shaw, the jeweller, and is a view looking up the street from the door of his shop. Clothing hanging up outside Thompson's the pawnbrokers is for sale, unredeemed pledges. The Bull's Head and Duke of Wellington Hotels are on the left side of the street. Mr. Alf Langley, landlord of the Duke of Wellington, was known as a very high class publican, serving his drinks in cut glass. Arthur Wellesley, the original 'Iron Duke', was of course of Wellington, Somerset. Although Mr. Shaw has taken his photograph carefully there is some 'fogging' due to the movement of people during the exposure. Mr. Willis' tobacconist shop is now a building society office and part of the original timbers in the wall next to Thompsons have been exposed.

33. Another framed 'Elite-Glazette' card from Milton shows New Street with Mr. Shaw's shop on the left and Willis and Co., tobacconist on the right. The card was posted in 1909 to a Miss N. Wellings in Nottingham. It is tempting to suggest that this may have been the lady who was designer to the Chad Valley Company and the Wrekin Toy Works in New Street and started her own doll factory after purchasing King Street Baptist Church in 1926. Thompson's pawnbroker sign shows clearly. It was a well-used shop with regular customers who pledged their belongings to obtain a cash loan. Unredeemed pledges were sold on the right hand side of the shop to cover the debt and many a bargain was purchased. Pawnbroking was strictly controlled by law.

34. The scene here is further up New Street and this is a rather earlier photograph. The horse and carriage probably belongs to Dr. Wedd, who had his surgery on the left. It seems about to turn through the archway towards the stables at the back of his house and the passenger looks very like the doctor. On the left side of the street the pair of little houses make a contrast with the taller, more elegant buildings of each side of them. For several years the end wall of the nearest one was exposed, showing its timber framing, before a new building, housing the unemployment benefit office, was completed. Higher up the street was an alley leading to Nailor's Row, a notorious slum where nail makers once lived, and further on was Chapel Lane, another slum area. The smart shops often concealed squalor behind them.

35. Looking down New Street we see on the right the shop of Keay, printers. James Keay was a printer in New Street in 1851 and the business continued until 1907 though Miss Keay sold stationery and foreign stamps for many years after that – certainly into the 1930's. An ancestor, William Keay, came to Wellington in 1811 from Shrewsbury and set up as a shoemaker. He joined the Baptist Church, became a Deacon and later Minister, and preached there for twenty years, though he continued his trade. The Keay family are commemorated in the name Keay Flats, a new development in High Street.

36. Again we are looking down New Street. On the left is the café of T. Sidoli, formerly the Shakespeare public house. Apart from keeping the café Mr. Sidoli, in the 1920's used to sell ice cream from a cart pulled by a small, slim horse which he drove round the town and the surrounding area, ringing a bell. He kept the ice cream in a churn with double walls, water being used as insulation. His cones were a penny and halfpenny each. The building on the right is the Duke of Wellington Hotel, then Latham's china shop and a passage, usually referred to as the Bull's Head yard, leading to the railway station. The shop marked Cornish advertises their trade as dyers, an occupation which had existed in Wellington since the early 14th century.

37. Looking down on New Street from a considerable height, one wonders what the photographer was standing on. Here the Bull's Head has been replaced by a new building containing the Bata shoe shop. On the left is the shop of York's, the local plumbers and engineers. Woolworth's, seen in the distance, sold many goods but had only two prices, sixpence and threepence. The shop on the left is having its front painted. This is a very ordinary, typical scene of a fairly busy day in the narrow main shopping street of a small town in the late 1920's. Most of the buildings, lower down the street at least, are still there but the businesses have changed hands.

38. New Street Methodist Church, shown here, was built in 1883 to the design of Herbert Isitt, seating 850. The imposing Italianate façade fronts a very plain building. There have been many Methodist churches in the town; this one was the last of several Wesleyan churches. There were also Primitive Methodist churches, the last of which, in Tan Bank, amalgamated with the Wesleyans of New Street and left their Tan Bank church to become a Muslim Mosque in 1978. Since this picture the interior of the church has been changed considerably; the galleries have been removed and the pews taken away and replaced by chairs so that the arrangement of seating is now flexible and the church can be more easily made informal. This building replaced an older Wesleyan chapel which since 1922 was the Chad Valley toy factory.

39. The photograph shows Sarah Smith, who was a very popular author under her pen name Hesba Stretton outside the old post office in New Street where her father was postmaster and bookseller. She wrote stories while still at school, but had not her sister, unknown to Sarah, sent one of them to Charles Dickens for his opinion, her work might never have come to light. Her pen name was derived from the initials of her brothers and sisters and a Shropshire village (Stretton). Her famous 'Jessica's First Prayer' was published in 1866 and sold 1½ million copies. Other works followed quickly. She helped found the London Society for the Prevention of Cruelty to Children which later became the N.S.P.C.C. 'Jessica's First Prayer' was translated into many languages and ordered by the Czar to be read in Russian schools.

40. Christ Church is seen here from Conduit Alley under which runs one of the many streams which come down from the Ercall. The church was built as a chapel of ease in 1839. The site on the south-east side of the town had been bought by the Church Building Commissioners from Lord Forester and building costs were £3,600, met by voluntary contributions and grants. The living was a curacy in the gift of the vicar of Wellington. The house to the left of the church is the old vicarage, now replaced by a house on the east side of the church. The terrace on the right of the church is older than the church itself. The culvert ran down Pool Head Lane, now Tan Bank. On the right are the grounds of the Vicarage of All Saints, later The Priory; the back gardens of houses in Rose-way stand there now.

41. Christ Church was designed by Thomas Smith of Madeley in the lancet Gothic style. It is of light yellow brick and resembles Smith's earlier church at Ironbridge. Originally it had a small recessed chancel, a nave with integral north and south aisles, a north lobby and a south vestry with a west tower. There is only one bell, dated 1838 named Great George and locally called 'the gruel bell' on account of its mournful note. The Reverend J.P. Abbey was vicar from 1913 to 1962 and changed its style from Evangelical to Anglo-Catholic. In nearly half a century as vicar he became very well known. Since his day the galleries have been removed; his ashes are intered within the church and his name has been given to Abbey Road.

42. The Old Hall, on Street Lane, has been associated with the Forester family at least since the 12th century. Forester is an occupational name; the family were hereditary wardens of the Forest of Mount Gilbert (The Wrekin) sometimes known as Wellington Haye. The building shown was commenced about 1480 by Edward Forester who built the two storey timber section parallel to Watling Street. The Foresters were at various times Lords of the Manor of Wellington. They moved to Dothill in 1648 and the present Lord Forester lives at Willey Park, Broseley. The right hand side or back of this house has been demolished and replaced by school buildings, only the part fronting Street Lane (now Holyhead Road) remains.

43. In the early 19th century Thomas Cranage leased the Old Hall from the Foresters and his wife Henrietta, a devout Quaker, started a school for girls there. This was continued by her daughter-in-law Martha until the famous Dr. Cranage opened a boys' school in 1845. He was an unconventional Anglican and, inspired by a visit to Ireland in 1859, led an undenominational mission among the poor of Wellington. He preached at the Town Hall and elsewhere, attracting numerous followers. In 1862 he built the New Hall, a large plain building off High Street. In 1889 a Children's Gospel Hall was added, partly with support from the Marchioness of Stafford. Cranage Crescent, off Hollies Road (formerly Slang Lane), commemorates the family name.

44. The Headmaster, Ralph Hickman, his staff and pupils of the Old Hall School are seen here in 1911. The school's founder, Dr. Joseph Edward Cranage, was headmaster for nearly fifty years, having opened the boys' school when he was only 19. He was inspired to do so after reading Dean Stanley's life of Dr. Arnold, the headmaster of Rugby. He succeeded in gaining an M.A. and Ph.D. from the University of Jena as an external student which was an outstanding achievement. He was headmaster of the Old Hall for nearly fifty years and his son took over in 1894, transforming it into a preparatory school for boys aged between eight and fourteen. Ralph Hickman was headmaster from 1906 to 1926.

45. The Buck's Head Hotel, seen here, was demolished in the early 1930's and replaced with a modern building. It is on the corner of Watling Street and Haybridge Road, originally in the township of Watling Street rather than Wellington. The field behind this hotel was used as a football pitch for many years by Wellington Town Football Club – known as the Lillywhites. Another team called Wellington Half Holiday, played at the same ground before the Great War. This latter team, composed mostly of apprentices, played on Wednesday afternoons. The people in the picture were probably members of the Peake family who kept the Buck's Head for many years.

46. This postcard shows the Baptist Church in King Street. The photograph was taken in 1910. the Baptist Church was formally established in Wellington in 1807 although it existed well before that date. A building on this site was registered as a Baptist Meeting House in 1809, demolished in 1828 and replaced by a larger building which was extensively renovated in 1880. In 1920 the Baptists joined with the Congregational Church and formed the Union Free Church on Constitution Hill. This Baptist Church was sold in 1929 to Nora Wellings becoming the Victoria Toy Works. The building was used as a doll factory for many years.

47. The New Secondary School shown here should actually be 'schools' as the building contained the Boys' and Girls' High Schools, very much two separate schools. Originally the Girls' High School opened in 1908 in the New Hall and transferred to the new premises in 1912 when there were places for 125 girls and 125 boys. Extensions were added at various dates to deal with constant overcrowding until by 1940 the boys moved to the Grammar School in Golf Links Lane and the girls took over the whole building. As seen, the building had the girls' school on the left of the central entrance and the boys' on the right. The hall was used for assemblies by both schools separately and as a gymnasium. Playgrounds in the rear were divided by a high wall. The girls played netball and hockey on ground to the north of the school while the boys' football and cricket ground was in New Church Road.

48. Wellington College, later Wrekin College, was founded in 1880 by Mr. (later Sir) John Bayley. When it was sold in 1920 by its founding principal it had 200 boys boarding. The name was changed to Wrekin College to distinguish it from Wellington, Somerset in 1921. This Frith's postcard shows the main part of the school in Sutherland Road in Edwardian times. It is an unusual view, showing the rear of the building across the playing fields presumably to get The Wrekin in the background. Although a monochrome photograph it has been hand coloured and given a sunset glow so nearly south as to be midwinter, contrasting with the summer vegetation.

49. Here we see a more conventional view of Wellington College taken from inside the Sutherland Road gates. The school has expanded; additional flat-topped dormers have enabled more accommodation to be built into the roof to sleep more boys. The central clock tower has also been added. Between 1880 and 1920 the school grew from one small house to a considerable college, due to John Bayley's energy and enthusiasm which earned him an enviable reputation as an educator. He was also active in the town, helping to expand the Services Club founded after the Great War into the Sir John Bayley Social Club. Sir John lived later at Buckatree Hall in some style and invested his money in land and property.

50. The Waterloo Hotel was built in Roslyn Road mainly to cater for parents visiting their sons in Wellington College. Its business was very seasonal and it was eventually taken over by the college and is now the headmaster's house. By 1903 Wellington College was the only boys' school in the town approved for county scholars, preparing candidates for county scholarships in secondary and higher education. Until it had its own chapel the boys attended services at New Street Methodist Church.

51. This Frith's postcard, posted in 1910 in Donnington, shows an earlier view of Wellington College before the clock tower was added. Sir John Bayley, the founder of the college, had been employed up to 1880 by the local School Board as master in Constitution Hill. After some dispute he left and started his own school, taking with him a few able pupils, Reverend Hamlet being one. He was involved in local politics with the Liberal Party. There is a local story that he challenged an irate parent to a boxing match in the gym. Various versions disagree as to who won the fight but all agree that mutual respect was the final result.

52. Hiatt's Ladies' College was founded in 1847 by Mrs. Elizabeth Hiatt, whose maiden name was Keay, as an independent day and boarding school for girls. By 1911 it had 15 teachers and was the largest of the three girls' schools in the town which were approved for county scholars. It closed in 1959, a year after the Girls' High School increased its intake. To the left of the picture is School House, the residence of the Headmistress and her solicitor husband. The buildings are now demolished but the school is commemorated by the name Hiatt Avenue, a residential street near the site of the school. Between 1909 and 1925 Miss Daniels was co-principal and bequeathed a sum of money to provide two scholarships. The aim of the school was to train girls to be good citizens and prepare them to take their place in the world.

53. The military parade shown in this old postcard took place on Armistice Day, 11th November, each year after the Great War. The photograph shows the King's Shropshire Light Infantry marching past a saluting base outside the Wrekin Hotel in the Square. The Lychgate War Memorial, built to commemorate the local men who had lost their lives in the Great War, can be seen near the centre of the photograph. The soldiers are carrying their Lee Enfield rifles 'at the trail' as was the custom of the Light Infantry who marched at a very fast pace. The policeman on the right is Sgt. 'Fatty' Whitby.

Series by the Scottish Photographic Touring and Pictorial Post Card Coy., Glasgow.

54. It was the custom for retailers to have postcards made of photographs showing their shops and staff. In fact the staff shown here was only part of the employees of this shop. There were many girls working in a workshop above the rear of the premises, busy with their needles and sewing machines producing most of the goods on sale. The date of this photograph appears to be around 1908 to 1910. With so many photographers in the town and firms such as Frith nationally one wonders why Mr. Capsey employed a Glasgow firm to produce his postcards. As will be seen, gentlemen's clothing was sold on the right of the shop and ladies on the left. The shop was in the Square and is also seen on photograph 7.

55. Mr. Baxter, whose shop is shown here, advertised his business on his gas lamps variously as hosier, draper and outfitter. As with Capsey's this shop had its gentlemen's department on the right, ladies on the left. In the 1920's Mr. Baxter used to stand just inside the doorway of his shop and call 'Forward' when a customer came in. There was a great deal of competition in his trade and service was a most important factor in attracting and keeping customers. In the centre of the shop was a large coke stove which warmed it in winter. The stove pipe went through the ceiling, heating the bedroom above. Mr. Baxter's daughter was a pharmacist and kept the Medical Hall in Church Street opposite the Charlton Arms Hotel.

56. Mr. Harvey can be seen here in front of his jewellers shop in Market Street. Like most jewellers at the turn of the century he was a watchmaker and optician as well as a jeweller. In addition to his business he was also a prominent local councillor. His work on the Housing Committee dealing with slum clearance and rehousing is commemorated by the name of Harvey Crescent. Like Mr. Capsey he has employed a Glasgow photographer to produce his cards. For many years the business was continued by Mr. Harvey's daughters.

57. Mr. A.E. Bloomer of Watling Street, Wellington, took this fascinating photograph of the peace celebrations to mark the end of the Great War. The photograph shows the interior of the Market Hall which has been cleared of its stalls to provide a huge refectory. A tea has been provided for the pupils of Wellington schools. Clearly the children are in their best clothes and on their best behaviour. The Market Hall was opened in 1868 by Wellington Market Hall Company who had acquired to the rights to market tolls from Lord Forester, the then Lord of the Manor. The hall's roof is supported by the cast iron columns seen in the photograph, which interestingly double as drain pipes taking water from the roof.

58. Outside the market hall in Market Street (formerly Butcher's Lane) can be seen the crowd waiting for the declaration of poll at the 1906 election. The results were as follows: C.S. Henry Lib. 4,806; H. Harmsworth Con. 3,114; liberal majority 1,692. Clearly the result has not yet been announced as there are no jubilant liberals. There are very few women in the waiting crowds, they had no vote until 1928. It was often said 'As The Wrekin, so the Country', so presumably there would have been a liberal government. To a large extent The Wrekin is still a marginal seat which serves as a barometer for the rest of the country. In fact at the time of this photograph Sir H. Campbell-Bannerman was liberal Prime Minister, to be followed in 1908 by Mr. Asquith.

59. The photograph was developed from a glass plate found in the effects of Mr. Shaw, the jeweller. It shows the outside of the market hall early on a Thursday morning. This part of the market was then called the potato market. Within the Market Hall, seen here on the left, were many permanent stalls. The potato market was reserved for farmers bringing vegetables and other produce to sell from their carts. In the background can be seen the Union Brewery and its chimneys. The left hand chimney belongs to the swimming baths.

60. The Smithfield livestock auction was photographed by Mr. A.E. Bloomer of Watling Street and shows local farmers gathered to form an association which eventually grew into the National Farmers' Union. The houses in the background are still standing and make it possible to identify the position of the photographer, looking towards the old cattle ring. Wellington was one of the first towns to have its own Smithfield livestock auction which was started in 1864 in the Bury Yards – where Victoria Avenue now is. It has remained in the control of Barber and Son who loaned this photograph. Cattle pens were incorporated into the railway goods station but animals were often driven to market and many a Monday was enlivened by stray, frightened beasts in the town.

61. The sepia photograph of this postcard can be easily dated as 1910 for it shows the opening of Wellington's first swimming baths. The building included slipper baths and the Superintendent's house. The pool remained much the same throughout sixty years of use, though the changing facilities were much altered. Until a filtration plant was installed in the 1950's the water was changed twice a week and charges reflected its purity – 6d., 4d., and 2d. On Saturdays the price was 2d., the bath was full of children and the water a very interesting colour. A special reservoir in the Limekiln Woods originally supplied the water. For most of its life the pool leaked and the underground passage around the bath became narrower as the walls were strengthened. Mr. Rogers, who was superintendent from 1911 to 1944, gave swimming lessons to men and boys while his wife taught girls and women. Changing cubicles were on the side of the bath and males and females had alternate times. The segregated swimming clubs were eventually merged.

62. Taken around the turn of the century, this photograph shows a double funeral, with two horse-drawn hearses lined up on Mill Bank. Mr. Harry Edwards, who founded the firm of undertakers, still operating in Wellington, is with the bearers, the third from the right. The first carriage was called the glass hearse; the second was a shillibier, which held the coffin in a glass case in front and seated eight mourners behind. Hearses and carriages were not owned by the undertaker but hired from the stables behind the Ercall Hotel, together with the horses. The procession would proceed at a slow walking pace to the cemetery. Mr. Edwards' father, Mr. Thomas Edwards, was a builder and undertaker. His brother Bill was in charge of the Fire Brigade. Mill Bank was so called because of the windmill which stood in nearby Mill Lane between the 14th century and the end of the 19th century.

63. In 1902 Wellington Urban District Council adopted the Public Libraries Act 1892 and was given the former Guardians' and Parish offices in Walker Street by H.H. France-Hayhurst of Overley Hall. A new front was built surmounted by an inscription commemorating the Coronation of King Edward VII. The houses on the left were demolished in the 1960's to make room for an extension. The building on the right, also formerly a part of the Union Workhouse, is now another extension. Before 1902 it was said that there was no reading room 'worthy of the name' but the new library had a lending library, reference department and reading room displaying local and national newspapers and magazines. The County Council took over the library in 1949.

64. This photograph shows part of the route for a celebratory parade to mark the coronation of King Edward VII. It is taken on the corner of Haygate, Wrekin and Bridge Roads with Walker Street on the right. Down Bridge Road is the Maltings used later by the Wrekin Brewery Company and now demolished. Broadway, the large house on the left, is now an office. The Queen's Head Hotel on the right still stands. Just beyond are the corrugated roofed sheds of John Bromley, the agricultural implement suppliers which were destroyed by fire in the 1950's. The Coronation was a welcome celebration after the mourning which followed the death of Queen Victoria.

65. Wellington had at least one fire engine in 1803, the vestry contributing to its maintainance. The brigade was controlled by the improvement commissioners from 1858 who opened a fire station in Walker Street in 1883. The engines were provided by the Alliance Assurance Co. In 1906 the brigade had eight operational members, all retained men. The Urban District Council bought a horse-drawn steam appliance in 1909 which is the one in the photograph. Mr. Edwards, seen here in his bowler hat taking charge of the brigade, is the brother of Mr. Harry Edwards, seen earlier supervising a funeral. The scene is in Haygate Road outside The Mount. The Urban District Council and Rural District Council formed the Wellington and District Joint Fire Brigade in 1928.

66. Haygate Road, shown here in the 1920's, had a sub-post office combined with a general stores. Lower down the road is the Bull Inn, Newtown which has now been demolished to make room for the Haygate Hotel. That part of Haygate Road was called New Town until fairly recently. It consisted of a collection of old cottages and shops built on land belonging to the Cludde family of Orleton Hall and may have been the resited village of Orleton, moved away from the Manor house in the 18th and 19th centuries. Haygate Road led originally to Wellington Haye – the Royal Forest, though it was formerly known as Shrewsbury Road past New Town.

67. The Cottage Hospital was built in 1912 in memory of J.C. Bowring under the will of his widow. It is in Haygate Road, near the Bowring Recreation Ground, opposite Bradley Moor. The hospital enabled local doctors to treat their patients in a surgery and was provided with wards and accommodation for nurses on night duty. Ownership passed from the trustees to the Regional Hospital Board in 1948. The postcard was published by Tom Austin, newsagent, Wellington whose descendants still keep the shop in High Street into which he moved in 1928.

68. The Gatehouse of Orleton Hall is of 16th century timber framed construction, jettied on all sides. There is a date 1588 in a chimney stack, though this probably refers to the rebuilding of an older structure, possibly of the same mediaeval date as the bridge across the moat. The remains of the moat are on the other side of the gatehouse; a short stretch of the original square moat which surrounded the hall. Orleton is an old house which was remodelled in 1830. The Cludde family of Cluddley lived at Orleton for many years until it passed to the Herbert family, related to the Earls of Powis. The present Earl was born at Orleton.

69. Mr. Bloomer's photograph shows the German aviator Gustav Hamel in a peaked cap with his back to the camera after landing his aeroplane in Orleton park in 1913. Colonel Herbert of Orleton is facing him with his walking stick. Mr. Harvey, seen earlier at his shop, is speaking from notes, no doubt on behalf of the local Council. The bearded gentleman in the cap is Mr. Gwynne of Haygate Farm. The small boy is Colonel Herbert's second son, known as Mr. Peter, and is now Earl of Powis. Nearest the camera is Reverend Turreff, Vicar of Wrockwardine, who was for many years a Rural District Councillor. On the right is Mr. Skitt reporting for the Wellington Journal.

70. The gazebo in the walled garden of Orleton Hall was built in the mid-18th century in the Chinese style. It has long been referred to as The Bothy but was not used for gardeners. The upper part was used on the 1920's as a summerhouse and the lower for a garden shed.

71. The panorama at the top of this composite picture looks very different now. The field in the right foreground is the Bowring Recreation Ground, given to the people of Wellington by John Crump Bowring who lived at Bradley Moor. On the left are the chapels of the cemetery – two separate chapels for different denominations on each side of the tower and spire. Most of the middle distance is now built up but The Ercall and The Wrekin remain much the same. The Wrekin Cottage and the Forest Glen Pavilion will be seen again later. The whole composition sums up well the relationship which has long existed between Wellington and the hills of The Wrekin for recreation.

72. The Red Lion Hotel on Holyhead Road (there is another Red Lion in Park Street) has now been plastered over its brickwork but otherwise looks much the same on the outside. Mr. Henry Pointon was the father of 'Ossie' Pointon and grandfather of Percy who kept the Forest Glen Pavilion under The Wrekin. The Pointon family were also plumbers, painters and decorators in Wellington.

73. Looking down from The Ercall, just above the old quarry, towards the north, the western part of Wellington lies below. The old quarry used to supply 'Ercall gravel' which was actually granophyre, a fine grained granite, and was used for garden paths and tracks. The large buildings in the middle of the picture comprised the new workhouse, or public assistance institution, built in 1876 in what was then called Street Lane, now Holyhead Road. It is now (since 1948) Wrekin Hospital. Most of the land between there and the woods is now built up. In the distance stretches the North Shropshire-Cheshire plain.

74. Looking from the summit of The Ercall towards The Wrekin this view is considerably different now. The hill in the foreground is Lawrence Hill (or St. Lawrence's Hill) and the valley between it and The Ercall has been extensively quarried and turned into a 'lunar landscape' to provide hardcore for the new town. The rock taken out was Wrekin quartzite (Cambrian). This view is used in the Geological Handbook of the Welsh Border together with a field sketch to show the rocks of The Wrekin. The track leading up from the Forest Glen to the summit can clearly be seen between the trees.

75. Wrekin Drive is now called Ercall Lane and is a favourite route for walkers between Wellington and The Wrekin. This was one of many Edwardian postcard views taken along this road. A great number of Wellington postcards show views of The Ercall and The Wrekin. Just beyond the young man in the photograph is now a bridge over the M54 motorway which is cut deeply into the Precambrian volcanic rocks of the Ercall hill.

76. Buckatree Hall was for many years the residence of Sir John Bayley, founder of Wellington College, after he had sold his school in 1920. It has for some years been a hotel. Behind the tree on the right is now a sunken concrete reservoir. On the left is now the entrance to a quarry. In the early 1850's Wellington Waterworks Company made its first reservoir called Ercall pools near Buckatree Hall, using a stream which passes under the road just where the furthest man is standing. It is now a pool in the hotel grounds. In 1859 a main descended from this reservoir, entering the town along Walker Street and terminating at a drinking fountain in The Square.

77. Further up Wrekin Drive (Ercall Lane) The Wrekin looms in front. The railings on the right are at the edge of the reservoir. Just around the corner to the left is the Forest Glen Pavilion. Until the motor car became common this road was thronged on public holidays and Sundays in the summer with walkers, carriages and horse – or motor-char-à-bancs. From all around Shropshire and from the Black Country trips were organised by churches, schools and clubs to The Wrekin. The Forest Glen and Wrekin Cottage did a very brisk trade and Mr. Sidoli of New Street would be there with his horse-drawn ice cream cart.

78. Posted in December 1906 this Valentines card shows the view across the fields and the reservoir to The Wrekin. The part of The Wrekin shown is in the Orleton estate. On the right can be seen the earth dam which held up the reservoir and the concrete spillway which channelled the overflow. The reservoir was supplied by a stream coming down the Forest Glen valley fed by springs on The Wrekin and in the Willowmoor Farm area to the south.

79. Looking from the earth dam of the reservoir; it is surprising that the photographer did not pick his day and light more carefully to ensure a reflection of The Wrekin in the water. From 1905 the waters of the stream were supplemented by water pumped from boreholes as the existing supply had proved to be inadequate. A main had been laid eastwards along Watling Street in the 1890's to extend the area supplied. Although the water is still there this reservoir is now used only as a fishing pool. All Wellington's water now comes from boreholes and is pumped into two covered reservoirs, one east and one north of the pool shown.

80. Mr. 'Billy' York is seen on the left of the picture in his 'plus fours' supervising the drilling of one of the boreholes which supplied water to The Wrekin reservoir. His brother Harold had a shop and a plumber's business in New Street and this photograph was rescued from the premises when the shop was demolished. The man on the left of the three was Bert Richards who used to play football at the Buck's Head in the 1920's for Wellington Town – the Lillywhites. Power for the drilling was supplied by the steam traction engine. Pipes were sunk into the triassic sandstone aquifer.

81. The Princess series of photographs were published by R.R. & S., Shrewsbury, so this is taken by a local photographer. The Forest Glen Pavilion was in the Pointon family for three generations and it was there in particular that the toast to 'All Friends Round The Wrekin' was proposed by the host. 'Ossie' Pointon and his son Percy kept the Forest Glen open for morning coffee and afternoon tea in the summer and it became a Mecca on weekends and holidays. It served mainly as a base from which people from Wellington and surrounding places, met and, suitably fortified, climbed The Wrekin. They also held dances and dinners in the evening. The char-à-bancs closed or open as seen here, brought passengers from Wellington Railway Station. The Pointon family lived in the house on the left. They amassed a great collection of the local Coalport china, now in the Ironbridge Museum.

82. This Valentines photograph taken at the turn of the century shows what is popularly called the Halfway House on The Wrekin. It provided a valuable pause for refreshment on the way up and down the hill. Miss Birrell, shown here, was famous for her ham and eggs and kept pigs and hens not far away. There were also donkey or pony rides for children and swing boats (often called swingle boats) to play on. Visitors could call in on the way up and order a cooked meal to be ready for them on the way down – after they felt they had earned it by their exertions. During The Wrekin Wakes in May this was the scene of much riotous behaviour at the fair where fights took place between colliers and yeomen for possession of the hill. These drunken battles caused the fair to be discontinued.

83. Hobson & Co., Market Square, Wellington, published this card. They were also printers but cannot have actually produced the cards themselves as this bears the legend 'printed in Saxony', in the rectangle marked 'affix half penny stamp'. In the Victorian and Edwardian days, before seaside holidays became more widespread and long before modern package air tours, an outing meant going up The Wrekin. Many people came from Birmingham, Wolverhampton and the Black Country to fill their lungs with good Shropshire air on The Wrekin. Often they came by train and char-à-banc in families, older members remaining at the Forest Glen, or climbing as far as the Cottage while the younger and more energetic walked to the top and joined the others on the way down.

84. Said at one time to have been caused by the same forces and at the same time as the renting of the veil of the temple – the moment of the Crucifixion – the Needle's Eye has always been a place of pilgrimage. Climbing through this narrow crack is supposed to be obligatory to all True Salopians. In pre-Christian times it may have been a centre for the Earth Mother religions. The accepted 'proper way' to go through is from south-west to north-east, i.e. the reverse of the way the Edwardian gentleman is facing. All things change and this little path in the foreground is now worn away. Other rocks on the south side of The Wrekin – The Cuckoo's Cup and the Bladder Stone are associated with old legends. There was reputed to be a hermit – at one time St. Gilbert – living in a cave near St. Hawthorn's Well. To reach the Needle's Eye the track from the Cottage enters an Iron Age hillfort through two gateways called Hell's Gate and Heaven's Gate.

85. Lilleshall Abbey was considered a suitable venue for day trips by carriage from Wellington. Holiday makers who could afford transport or walkers at the end of Queen Victoria's reign and later would journey to see the Abbey ruins. It was founded by Augustinian canons from Dorchester around 1148 and used by them until surrendered to the Crown in 1538. Subsequently a Wolverhampton wool merchant, James Leveson, bought the manor. The Leveson-Gowers owned it for some time, later Granville, Marquess of Stafford and Duke of Sutherland. During the Civil War Lilleshall was garrisoned for the Crown but fell to Parliament in 1645 after a long resistance. Nearby Lilleshall Hall once catered for char-à-banc parties from Birmingham and elsewhere and had a toy railway to the Abbey ruins.

86. The remains of Much Wenlock Abbey are in the foreground of the picture with the town's Church in the background. The Abbey or Priory was established as a nunnery in AD 680 by Milburga, daughter of Merewald, King of Mercia but destroyed by the Danes in 896. It was later re-founded by Roger de Montgomery, first Earl of Shrewsbury, who held Wellington in the Domesday survey. The ruins are still impressive and are now cared for by the Department of the Environment. From Wellington, Much Wenlock would have required a full day out, crossing the River Severn by the iron bridge or by train across the Albert Edward bridge and up Farley Dingle. This was a delightful train journey which is sadly now impossible as the railway is closed.

87. The iron bridge, now so famous internationally, was regarded merely as one of the places worth a visit when staying in Wellington. It was a short journey by train or by carriage down Jigger's Bank. For most of its history the iron bridge was a toll bridge until taken over by the County Council. The house on the left of the bridge was the toll house. Surprisingly the picture shows no river traffic of the Severn trows nor coracles out fishing. At one time Ironbridge and Coalbrookdale were the leading industrial sites in the country if not in the world. The bridge was built in 1779 by Abraham Darby III though its instigation was partly due to John Wilkinson of Broseley who also launched the first iron boat.

88. Coalbrookdale, in the picture, has the Coalbrookdale works of the Darby family in the foreground making so little smoke that it must be Sunday. On the right is Paradise with the Coalbrookdale Institute in the middle distance. Further away to the left is the Church, given by the Darby family. The background trees are in Dale Coppice. Throughout the 18th, 19th and early 20th centuries Coalbrookdale was a hive of industry, producing iron goods, especially castings of great variety. Later it declined, not being able to compete until recently when it became a tourist spot. Abraham Darby bought a charcoal/iron furnace here in 1709 and pioneered the use of coke instead of charcoal. Iron ore, coal (for coking) and limestone (for flux) were combined to produce cast iron goods of many kinds – often newly invented. Raw materials were brought down into the valley whose stream supplied water power.

89. The Roman-British City of Viroconium Cornoviorum or Uriconium was the capital of the Cornovii tribe, previously administered from The Wrekin hillfort. It has been suggested that Saxon mercenaries who lived here founded the weoleah (sacred grove with a heathen temple) which developed into Wellington. The Old Work, the large ruin here, was the wall of the public baths. There have been excavations on this site for many years; stones were removed to build nearby churches and Thomas Telford removed a mosaic when rebuilding Shrewsbury Castle. Archaeological investigations were begun seriously by the Shropshire Archaeological Society in the 1870's. The site now belongs to the Department of the Environment.